LittleMissMatched's

the writer in me!

How to Write Like Nobody Else!

WORKMAN PUBLISHING • NEW YORK

Library of Congress Cataloging-in-Publication Data

Littlemissmatched.
Littlemissmatched's the writer in me! : how to write like nobody else!
p. cm.
ISBN-13: 978-0-7611-4764-0 (alk. paper)
1. Authorship. I. Title. II. Title: Writer in me!
PN147.L58 2007
808'.02—dc22   2007042561

Design by Barbara Balch
Illustrations by Holly Kowitt

Workman books are available at special discounts when purchased
in bulk for premiums and sales promotions as well as for fund-raising
or educational use. Special editions or book excerpts also can be
created to specification. For details, contact the Special Sales
Director at the address below.

Workman Publishing Company, Inc.
225 Varick Street
New York, NY 10014-4381
www.workman.com

Printed in China
First printing February 2008
10 9 8 7 6 5 4 3 2 1

acknowledgments

I wanna thank all the fabulous, marvelous, kooky, zany people who helped make *The Writer in Me!* possible. They are: my bestest book doctor, nurse, and midwife, David Henry Sterry; my illustrator extraordinaire, Holly Kowitt; my research maestros, Joey Bacal and Jessica Bacal; my high priestess of poetry, Tina Jacobson; my writer goddess Susan Wooldridge; my raja of reporting, Danielle Svetcov; my most excellent editor, Eva Steele-Saccio; my exceptional conspirator and fast friend, Raquel Jaramillo; my fantastic fairy godmother, Suzie Bolotin; my masters of marketing and publicity, Kim Small, Andrea Fleck, and Jessica Varon; my ATF COO, Walter Weintz; my distinguished professor of publishing, Peter Workman; my graphic design diva, Barbara Balch; my queen of details, Katherine Camargo; my all-around handy helper, Kristen Culp; my color coordinator, Penelope Horcha; my style maven and Gal Friday, Aimee DeLong; and my constant source of inspiration, Chile Pepper.

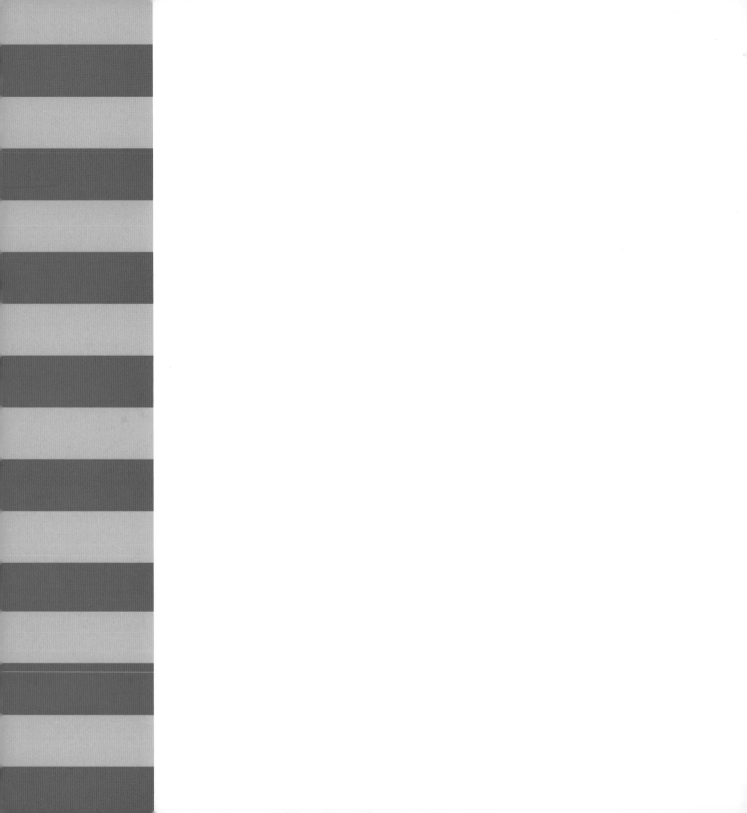

contents

so you wanna be a writer?

"I think I did pretty well, considering I started out with nothing but a bunch of blank paper." —Steve Martin, Actor and Writer

Hi, I'm LittleMissMatched, and I love to write. Anything and everything: short stories, poems, plays, screenplays, articles for my school newspaper, journal entries about stuff I did during the day, and just plain gobbledygook.

I don't know why, but I've always made up stories. Sometimes about people I know, and sometimes about people I've never met but I'd like to meet. Sometimes I write stories about people I totally make up. One of my favorite feelings is when I finish a story and give it to one of my friends, and she starts talking about the characters like they're real people. Then I know I have a really good story on my hands. But I also like writing about creatures from other worlds— house-elves and hobgoblins, or mythological creatures like fairies, flying horses, lions, and pigs. Cuz sometimes I just wanna go to a world far, far away.

I've also been writing poetry since I was really little—or at least my parents called it poetry. My first poems were pretty silly. I know, because I have the first poem I ever wrote. See, my dad sent it in to a magazine that his company puts out every month, and it got printed on the page they have about the kids of people who work there. So . . . drum roll . . . here's the poem:

My Kat

My kat
Is fat
Fat fat fat fat fat fat fat
Kat kat kat kat kat kat kat

What can I say? I was only five years old. Luckily, my poems are much better now. And I write tons of them. What's great about poetry is that you can write a whole poem in just five minutes, or you can work on one for months if you feel like it.

And there are all different kinds of poems, too. One of my favorites is the haiku. It's a short, three-line poem that was invented in Japan, and it's really fun to write because you have to follow a bunch of rules but you can still be wild 'n' wacky. And I also really love to write spoken-word poetry. That's poetry where you rhyme all the time—if I'm lyin', I'm dyin'.

One of the reasons I adore spoken-word poetry (which is also called performance poetry) is that it's meant to be said out loud. There are even spoken-word poetry competitions called "slams," where people get together and perform their poems in front of an audience and judges. One by one, the poets get eliminated, until there's a champion. And then the local champions compete against each other until finally, at the end, there's a national champion.

Last year I got to perform at a poetry slam, and OMG it was so amazingly amazing. I didn't win, but I didn't care because it was just so much fun to be up there performing. It felt so cool because everybody was all quiet when they were listening to me. And, oh man, afterwards everyone clapped and whistled. Plus it was really excellent to see all these other poets—some of them were sooooo great. It made me wonder why people don't go to poetry slams as often as they go to the movies.

After I started writing short stories and poetry, I decided I wanted to try out writing other stuff, too. So I gave plays a try. I've written a bunch so far. My favorite one is about the most

normal family in the world, except for the fact that the mom is a spy. My friends and I put it on for the talent show at camp, and we wore lots of crazy costumes and wigs and mustaches. We even wrote a song for it. It was so much fun, we laughed ridiculously hard! Even my big sister said it was good, and she basically hates everything I do. (Well, that's not totally true, I guess it just seems that way.) Anyway, we still quote lines from that play to this day.

Then last year, I wrote a few of my very own screenplays (most of them are only a page or so long, but still!). Then I made movies outta them with my best friend, Jasmine. I think the best one is a vampire movie with my cat Chile Pepper. She's a total movie star and can really flaunt her stuff.

I also write in my journal ALL THE TIME! The amazingly great thing about a journal is that you can carry it with you wherever you go. You don't have to worry about forgetting any brilliant ideas while you're waiting for the bus or in line at the library, because you can jot anything down as soon as you think of it. You can also put your journal on the nightstand next to your bed, so you can write down your crazy dreams when you wake up and they're still fresh. Whenever I'm feeling really stressed or upset or mad cranky and I write about it in my journal, I always feel better. Or, if I'm confused about something and I write about it, by the time I get done alotta times I've figured out the problem.

Like one time I got invited to two separate parties for two different friends of mine, and the parties were at the same time! I didn't know which one to go to, and I was mega-stressed. I talked to EVERYONE about the decision, but I *still* couldn't figure out what to do. Then I went and wrote about it in my journal, and by the time I finished, it was sooooooo obvious that I could divide my time and go to *both* parties! I'm always amazed at how much more clearly you see things when you write them down. And later, when you look back at old journal entries, you can remember exactly what you were thinking or doing. It's pretty crazy to see how your brain works and to read about things you completely forgot happened.

I've also gotten really into being a reporter. And the crazy thing is, it was totally by accident. See, three months ago, I got obsessed with a certain type of stickers—these mini Japanese characters with zany colored clothes and hair. There's this one store where practically everyone in town buys their stickers and school supplies. But one day, when I went in, they didn't have the stickers. When I asked the owner if she could order them, she totally blew me off. So I went online and I found 'em in about three secs. The website that sold the stickers also had all these school supplies that we normally buy from the store I was telling you about. Only they cost like half as much. I was soooooooo shocked. I called a dozen other stores, too.

And no one charged nearly as much as the store in my town.

While I was investigating, I decided I wanted to write an article about this for my school newspaper. So I did! I interviewed all these different people and did a whole bunch more research to get my facts straight. It was like being a detective in a movie or something. And it was so cool when I finished the story because I totally proved that you could get all your school supplies for so much less than people were used to paying—and get some really cool stickers at the same time!

Whew! As you can see, I've done my fair share of writing lately. And I've learned A TON of awesome things that have helped me become a better writer. So instead of keeping it all to myself, I thought I'd share it with you, since you also love to write. And after you read this book and do the activities inside with the space provided, you'll be able to write like nobody else but your fabulous, marvelous self!

chapter one:
the short-story writer
in me

If you wanna be a writer, my guess is you also like to read. I personally love, love, love that feeling of getting under the covers, opening the pages of an awesome book, reading until I can't keep my eyes open, and then dreaming I'm in the book itself. And I happen to be a particular fan of novels and short stories.

One summer, my best friend, Jasmine, and I had a contest to see who could read the most books.

Jasmine won—she read twenty-eight! But I read twenty-one, which I thought was pretty cool. My parents, my English teacher, Ms. Radcliffe, and practically everyone I met thought it was amazing that Jasmine and I read so many books. But what's funny is that after that summer, Ms. Radcliffe told us that novels and short stories (or "tales," as they were called back in the day) used to be considered something to turn your nose up at. Like people actually believed it was low-class or even gross to read a novel or short story. It wasn't until the nineteenth century that novels and short stories were thought of as real art—and reading them was considered a good thing.

Weird, huh? I think it's way strange because, if you think about it, people are telling stories all the time, and they have been forever. In fact, Ms. Radcliffe said that part of what makes us human is that we can tell stories, because other animals can't. Just take any normal day. If you listen, you'll hear stories all around you, all the time. Like maybe a kid sitting in front of you tells the guy next to him a story about how he almost missed the bus, and he had to run with all his might

to catch it. Or maybe your best friend tells you a story in science class about how she accidentally took her mom's wallet to school and what her mom had to go through to pick it up right before a totally important meeting. Maybe when you get home, your sister tells you a story about how a girl she doesn't like at school was wearing the exact same shirt AND shoes and how they got into a crazy fight about it.

So what exactly is a story, anyway? What makes it different from a conversation or, say, a few sentences strung together? For one thing, any story worth its salt has a beginning, middle, and end. Like I have this one friend who is really, really nice. But she makes you crazy because right after she starts a story, she goes off in like nineteen different directions, and you have no idea what she's talking about. I won't mention her name, of course, but seriously, her stories are the worst! In fact, I'm not even sure you can call them stories, exactly, because they so

DON'T have a beginning, middle, or an end. They're just alotta hot air, if you ask me.

Okay, so a story has to have a beginning, middle, and end. But what makes a story totally, fabulously, marvelously excellent? One of my ATF awesome stories is *The Wonderful Wizard of Oz*. If you think about it, you'll remember that all the main characters in this story have terrible problems. They all want something really, really bad. Like the only thing Dorothy wants is to go back home to Kansas (which I can totally relate to because one time I got lost in the mall, and I seriously thought I would never see my room, or my house, or my cat, or my mom, or my dad, or my sister ever again—it was so scary!). The Cowardly Lion wants courage so bad, it makes him cry. The Tin Man wants a heart so bad, it paralyzes him. And the Scarecrow wants a brain so bad, he falls apart.

The fact that they each want something so desperately makes you, the person reading the story, want them to get whatever they need. Like if Dorothy doesn't make it back to Kansas, she'll never ever, ever, ever see her wonderful aunt and uncle again—and that would be completely heartbreaking. So you're rooting for Dorothy to get back home. But what else makes a great story? When I read my twenty-one books, I took some notes, and this is what I came up with:

❀ An amazing setting. When you read a story, you wanna enter the world of the main character. And there's no better example than Oz! With Munchkins, a yellow brick road, flying monkeys, an emerald city, good and bad witches, it's a truly amazing world that is super-exciting to read about.

❀ Other interesting characters who also have problems or things they want, and who try to help the main character get what she has her eye on. Think about the Tin Man, the Cowardly Lion, and the Scarecrow.

❀ Lots of really difficult obstacles your heroine has to overcome to get what she wants. Like Dorothy has to get the broomstick from the Wicked Witch of the West, and it only just happens to be the witch's most prized possession.

❀ A villain who tries to stop the main character from achieving her goal. *The Wonderful Wizard of Oz* has an amazing villain: the Wicked Witch of the West. And she keeps doing evil stuff to Dorothy, like trying to kill her—over and over and over again.

❀ Suspense. You totally can't wait to see what happens next, and you just wanna keep turning the page, even if it's so late you're falling asleep as you read.

❀ Satisfaction. You gotta feel fullfilled at the end of the story, like you've taken this amazing trip with the characters. And while you're totally bummed that the story is over, you can't wait to tell all your friends about the ending.

No matter how short or long your story is (you might even wanna write a novel some day!), if you include the stuff I talked about, you've got a good shot at writing a totally, fabulously, marvelously excellent story.

One of the great things about a short story is that it's short. You can read a whole story on a Sunday afternoon, and you can write one in a weekend. I know, cuz I've done it a lot. But you can also work on a short story for a whole year if it toots your horn. In fact, I've been writing, and rewriting, and rewriting one short story called "Mousse in My Face" for like three whole years now. At first I called it "Rhubarb Pie on My Head." Then I changed it to "Coconut Cream Pie in My Eye." And after that, I decided on "Custard Pie up My Nose." That's how it is with stories. Sometimes they come out easily, but other times you have to write them over and over and over 'til you get them right.

Short stories can be sad or happy, scary or safe, funny or serious, sweet or creepy, exciting or calm, old-fashioned or set in the future. You can write short stories about your friends, or your family, or your pets, or stuff that happens to you, or stuff you wish would happen to you, or stuff you wish would never happen to you. Or you can make anything up using your crazy imagination. So here are some activities that will help you get started.

ACTIVITY 1:

Picture That

I found an old photograph my mom took before I was born of my first cat, Jumbo—the one that died when I was three. He's lying across a radiator, looking off into space. His paw is hanging over the edge. And the leaves of a plant are draped on his shoulder. A glass jar of dried roses is next to his head. Jumbo was just a young cat when my mom took the picture. But for some reason, the photo looks sad, and when I first saw it, it made me think about when he died.

So I decided to write a short story using this picture. I used all the details of the photo—the stuff I already mentioned, plus what the light looked like and how it made his body kind of glow. But I pretended it was Jumbo's very last day on this earth. Somehow, all the stuff in the photograph helped me imagine what that time might have been like for him.

Photos can be a great way to jump-start your imagination or

"**Finding the right form for your story is simply to realize the most natural way of telling the story. The test of whether or not a writer has divined the natural shape of his story is just this: After reading it, can you imagine it differently, or does it silence your imagination and seem to you absolute and final? As an orange is final. As an orange is something nature has made just right.**" —Truman Capote, Writer

blast you into a world that you may totally know—or even one you don't know at all. Pull out some of your own pictures. Old family photos, vacation snapshots, photos of your friends. Or, look in magazines for people or places that interest you. Describe the scene: What do you see? What do you smell? What do you hear?

Get into the nitty gritty. Like is there a purple stain on someone's white shirt? Is there a yummy barbecue smoking in the background? Is a bird flapping its wings in the distance? Once you've got the setting down, then choose a character—maybe someone in the photo, or maybe a person who you imagine walking into the picture a couple minutes later. Think about what happens next, and take it from there!

ACTIVITY 2:

Capturing Character

At the beginning of *The Catcher in the Rye* (which is one of my ATF books), Holden Caulfield—the hero of the book—describes his dorm room at school. He talks about this guy Ackley who is clipping his toenails on Holden's dorm room floor. The description is so good, it makes you wanna scream at the guy yourself. You just wanna be like, "That's so totally gross! Get outta my room!!!"

The way you describe characters and what they're doing, whether they're real people, or people you're just making up, will go a long way toward making your writing mad interesting—or super-boring. It's really, really important to learn how to write about people so that when somebody reads your description, they're interested enough in your characters to wanna read more. And the more you practice describing people (all the different parts of their personalities, their good points and bad points, what they look like, what they talk like, what they dress like, what they do when they walk in a room), the better you'll get at it.

Take some time to really listen to a conversation. It can be anywhere. It can be between people you know or don't know. Try to write down at least a few lines of exactly what each person is saying. Pay super-close attention to each person's body language during the conversation, too. Do one person's hands move a lot? Does the other person curl up the edge of her mouth? Does she keep tugging at her shirt or skirt because she's nervous? Be sure to write this stuff down as well.

Now write a bigger dialogue that uses the piece of conversation you recorded. Break up the talking by describing what the characters do and look like. You'll be amazed to see how all the rest of the dialogue—and the story— that you make up will sound much more real!

keepin' it real

When you read a story by Eudora Welty, you feel like the characters and the place that she wrote about are really real. I think part of the reason is that she wrote about what she knew—people and places from the Mississippi Delta, where she grew up and lived her whole life. Eudora uses all these little phrases that are only used in that part of the world. And, let me tell you, they've got a funny way of talking. Like when someone hears something that seems strange, they might say, "Well I declare!" Anyway, her writing makes characters you've never seen or heard before (unless you happen to live there, too) come to life, flesh and blood before you.

But at the same time, her stories are about things we can all relate to. You totally know how the characters are feeling, you've done the same things they have, and you've had to make similar decisions. Reading Eudora's stories feels familiar and new all at once. One of the reasons she's so good at making you feel this way is that she listened really hard and paid really close attention to the people around her—how they talked and acted and what they said. In her book *One Writer's Beginnings,* Eudora talks about how when she was a kid, she was so into listening to other people's conversations that when she got into the car with her mom and some friends, she'd beg them to tell her stories, the juicier the better. Luckily, I don't have that problem with my mom and sister because they *love* to talk—which is great cuz I can use everything they say in my stories.

So I say be like Eudora and listen when people are gossiping on the phone, chitchatting in the cafeteria, or telling crazy stories at your next visit to the hair salon. Where are they from? Do they talk softly or loudly? What are they taking about? Do they show their emotions? What makes them unique? Record **EVERYTHING** and then get cracking on your own realer than real story.

ACTIVITY 3:
Getting All Emotional

One of the greatest short-story writers ever is Edgar Allan Poe. He lived in the nineteenth century and was one of the first people who said that short stories were art. And he had alotta incredibly incredible rules about short stories. One of his rules was that every short story should be about one emotion. Like in his famous story "The Tell-Tale Heart," Edgar wrote about guilt. See, it's a story about a guy who kills an old man for no good reason at all, just because he doesn't like the old man's eye. But then he starts to feel really, really guilty—so guilty that when the police arrive, he starts hearing the dead dude's heart pounding underneath the floor where he was buried. It's creepy and spooky, but it really shows you what guilt can do.

Now take a page outta Edgar Allan Poe's book. Pick an emotion—happiness, sadness, jealousy, fear, joy, whatever— and write a story that revolves around it. You can even start the story here.

_____

_____

_____

_____

_____

_____

_____

_____

_____

_____

_____

_____

_____

_____

_____

_____

ACTIVITY 4:
Odd Jobs and Actions

If you wanna read a bunch of excellent books about a cool job, you gotta check out James Herriot's stories. My favorite is *All Creatures Great and Small*.

James was a veterinarian who lived in a small town in England. He looked after all kinds of animals, and he met lots of amazing people who lived in his town or owned the animals that he cared for. So James wrote incredible stories about his job—what went on with the cows, pigs, and sheep, as well as the owners (who, alotta times, were even crazier than the animals).

Anyway, it's really fun to mix 'n' match (or mismatch!) jobs and actions to see what story jumps outta these combinations. All you have to do is write down five jobs on different slips of paper. Stuff like "veterinarian," "teacher," "ice-cream server," "airline pilot," or "wizard."

Now write down five actions on five more slips of paper. Stuff like "surfing a wave," "walking the dog," "making a mess," "getting struck by lightning," "washing the dishes." Put the jobs into one pile and actions into another. Mix the slips in each pile. Now pick one slip from each category. Write a sentence that puts the two together, and use it to start a most excellent story.

ACTIVITY 5:
Hearing Voices

The other day I read a short story by Eudora Welty called "Why I Live at the P.O." Eudora wrote the story when she was an adult, but I swear, the main character, who tells the whole story, sounds exactly like my friend Lisa, who is my age. The way the words come outta her mouth and how the character speaks are really unique and interesting, and you feel like you can hear her talking in real life. In proper writing terms, this is called the "voice" of the story. All stories have a voice, even if it doesn't jump out at you. Sometimes, you'll start dreaming in that voice, it's so strong.

A good way to learn how to write with a strong voice is to start noticing real people's voices. Like I have one friend who ends all her sentences as if she's asking a question—her voice just kinda goes up at the end in a funny way.

She'll say to me, "I really like your socks?" Then I have another friend who talks so fast allherwordsrun togetherintoonebigword. I also have a teacher who starts all her sentences in a loud voice, but then gets all quiet at the end. **"Please turn in your homework** by 2 P.M. tomorrow." And Jasmine's dad has a cool accent because he's from Senegal, a country in Africa where people speak French. He never pronounces the "h" at the beginning of a word. Like he'll say, "'ow are you? Is your 'ouse okay? Are you still 'aving problems with your 'amster?"

Is there someone you know with a unique voice? A doctor, say, who talks too loud? A classmate, like, who says "like," like, every other word? A grandparent who always seems to pause mid-sentence and then begins the sentence all over again and again and again? After you've found this person, try to write in his or her voice. Choose a topic he or she would care about and write some stylin' stuff this character might say.

chapter two:

the poet in me

People have been popping out poems for thousands and thousands of years. Back in the day, because most people couldn't read, poems were always recited. Probably the most famous poems like this are the *Iliad* and the *Odyssey,* which were written by the ancient Greeks thousands of years ago. We're talking somewhere between the eighth and sixth centuries B.C.

The *Iliad* tells the story of the Trojan War, the most famous war in ancient Greece. There are tons of super-gory battles, a crazy kidnapping, and a gigantic wooden horse that is given as a gift but actually has soldiers hidden inside. The *Odyssey* tells the story of Odysseus—a hero from the Trojan War—and his super-long journey back home. On his way, he visits the land of the lazy Lotus-eaters, escapes a one-eyed monster called the Cyclops, and is tempted by the magical songs of the Sirens.

One of the things I learned from reading lots of different kinds of poems is that they can be about

didya know?!

For many, many years, people said the *Iliad* and the *Odyssey* were written by a guy named Homer—a man who was blind and couldn't read or write. But now, historians think that these poems were probably written by more than one person, and maybe even alotta people. You see, the *Iliad* alone has 15,693 lines. That's hours and hours worth of poetry, which would be pretty hard for one dude to make up and memorize all by himself!

almost anything and everything. They can be about things that really happened or things you completely make up. They can be really long or really short, totally serious or seriously silly. They can rhyme all the time. Or not. Ever. There are happy poems, sad poems, peace poems, war poems, love poems, animal poems, story poems, and nonsense poems. People write poems all over the world. And when you think about it, songs are really poems set to music. Rock songs, pop songs, folk songs, Broadway musicals, and rap—they are all types of poetry! Another most excellent thing about poems is that you can perform them. It can be crazy fun to read a poem in front of people or watch someone really talented perform her poetry.

One time I went to a poetry reading at the library, and all these poets got up and read. The poetry reading was an "open mike" and all you had to do was sign up on a list, and you got to read your poems for five minutes! The first person to read was a woman with kooky, beautiful red hair. She had lotsa scarves on, and amazing bracelets that rattled when she got all excited. She read an awesomely awesome poem about her horse. I'll never forget it. The horse's name was

Charcoal. And when the woman described what the horse looked like and how it ran, it was almost like you were riding the horse with her. In the end, poor Charcoal broke his leg, and they had to put him to sleep, and I started crying, I swear. When I looked around, lots of other people were crying, too. I thought it was totally, totally amazing that one poem could make so many people feel the same way.

Since then, I've been trying to write a poem like that, one that really gets to people. And in the meantime, I've been having tons of fun exploring all kinds of poetry. I'll tell you all about it. . . . Ready to get your poetry groove on?

ACTIVITY 1:
Wild Word Collecting

Words are the most incredibly incredible things. There are so many of them, and lots of them mean different stuff depending on how you use them. The way I look at it, the more words you know, the better you can tell people what you think, what you feel, and what you want—and the better a writer you'll be.

Words are kind of mysterious; their meanings and spellings change all the time, and yet lots of them are thousands and thousands of years old (I like learning about the history of words while I'm looking something up in the dictionary). And then there are some words that were just invented recently. Like the word *blog*. That word didn't even exist in the twentieth century. But, now, it seems like everyone but my cat Chile Pepper has a blog, and even she's about to get hers up and running.

Collecting words is one of my favorite ways to get inspired to write poetry. You can collect words wherever you go. From billboards and street signs to magazines and books—always be on the lookout for a new and cool word. And if

lovin' the lingo

Here are some of my favorite words: wigwam, mom, pom-pom, bat, cat, hat, chitchat, mustard, custard, chicken, fingerlickin', stringy, thingy, spifferific, peppercorn, born, horn, hootenanny, uncanny, cutlet, piglet, crab apple, dapple.

there's no word for something, you can make up your own. I do it all the time. Like one night my sister was going out. She looked incredibly amazing and all put together, but there wasn't one word that perfectly described her. So I made up the word *spifferific*. She looked *spiffy* and *terrific*. Spifferific! Lewis Carroll, who wrote two awesome books, *Alice's Adventures in Wonderland* and *Through the Looking-Glass* (most people read them together and call them *Alice in Wonderland*), used to invent words all the time. He even made up the word *chortle*, which combines the words chuckle and snort. If you say it a couple of times, it's kinda funny, cuz it actually sounds like a chortle.

So start writing down your favorite words on the blank cards that come in this kit. Then put them in the "wild word" box (also in the kit). The more interesting, nutty, crazy, kooky, mad, and phantasmagorical words you collect, the better.

Now, are you ready to write a poem? Take out a dictionary, or your favorite novel, or even a cookbook. Close your eyes, open the book randomly, and put your finger on a word. Now open your eyes and write the word down on another blank card. (If you run out of cards, you can also use slips of paper.) Do this as many times as you want, and when you have ten or fifteen interesting words, start mixing and matching them with the words you already have in your "wild word" box. Have you found some funny, kooky, zany combinations? Like a "stretchy computer," a "pomegranate hamburger," or a "finger nugget"? Interesting word combinations are most excellent starting points for poems. Use one of these combinations in your first line. If you like, use other combinations, too, or just see where your imagination takes you!

didya know?!

"Assonance" and "alliteration" are two cool tools to use when you're building a poem. Assonance is when two or more words have vowel sounds that are the same. Like: The brown hound was found around the downtown pound. Alliteration is when two or more words have consonant sounds that are the same. Like: The kooky cat cooked crazy cucumber-crab cupcakes.

ACTIVITY 2:
To Rhyme or Not to Rhyme

Rhyming can be a ton of fun, but you don't wanna have to rhyme all the time. The first poems I remember are by Dr. Seuss, and they had really simple rhymes that are easy to say—*two* and *blue, cat* and *hat,* stuff like that. But there are really complicated rhymes, too. Like in *The Wonderful Wizard of Oz,* the Cowardly Lion sings a song, and he rhymes the word *brontosaurus* with *king of the forest.* I totally love that rhyme!

Now, take five of your favorite words from your "wild word" box and write two different poems that use *all five words* (and any others you want). Write one poem that rhymes and one that doesn't. Did having to rhyme cramp your style or did it loosen you up? Compare the poems side by side. Which one do you like better? Why?

Slammin' and Jammin' in Your Neighborhood

One of the things I like most about poetry is that it is full of different rhythms. Some poems have a steady beat, some jump all over the place, and some move really slooooooooooooow. The rhythm of a poem depends on where you put your emphasis on each word. Like this poem by Gelett Burgess:

The Purple Cow

I never saw a purple cow,
I never hope to see one;
But I can tell you, anyhow,
I'd rather see than be one.

If you tap your foot when you recite the poem, you can hear the rhythm. Where you put the emphasis is called a beat. To me, the beats in "The Purple Cow" are on *never* and *purple*, *never* and *see*, *I* and *anyhow*, and *rather* and *be*. Are you with me?

Now go stand outside somewhere. In your yard, on a street corner, in the schoolyard during recess. Totally listen, really carefully. You'll be amazed by all the rhythms around you. A bird chirping. A train rushing by. A basketball dribbling. Make notes in your journal (one comes with this kit) about the stuff you see around you and the rhythms that you hear. Then, later, when you have some peace and quiet, come back to this page and write a poem about what you saw. Try to make it have the rhythm that you heard. Then read your poem out loud. If you feel like it, imagine that you're performing it in front of a bunch of people, like at a poetry slam.

hard in the schoolyard

One day at school during recess, I looked and listened to everything around me. The rhythms in the schoolyard were kinda harsh and strong. I wrote down all these words in my notebook: *schoolyard, hard, asphalt, tar, hoops, chatter, traffic, train tracks, airplane, shouts, screams, shuffle, chitchat, bouncing ball, whistle, chant, rant, plant, jump rope, slap, fast, pound, foot, hand.* Then some boys started picking on me. I went home and wrote a poem about what happened using the words I'd written down. I tried to capture the same rhythms that I heard on the schoolyard in my poem. Here it is:

hard in the schoolyard

*sometimes it gets hard
in the schoolyard,
when you got no bodyguard
and the tar is hot and the bully boys
aren't gonna leave you alone
and you wanna go home*

*or get on the phone
and try a cry for help or go inside
but there's no place to hide
when it gets hard in the schoolyard
and you got no bodyguard
so you duck and shuffle,
shuffle and duck,
but you have no luck
and you're stuck
are you gonna tattle
when you get rattled?
does it matter
if you tell the powers that be,
hey, they're picking on me,
why's everybody always picking on me?
without a doubt i wanna shout out,
cut it out, cut it out, cut it out
instead i'll write it here
cuz i don't want a kick in the rear
but here's a word to the wise:
pick on somebody your own size
and then maybe it won't be so hard
in the schoolyard
when you got no bodyguard*

ACTIVITY 4:
Change the World

There's this excellent tradition in poetry where people try to make the world a better place by writing a poem. One of my dad's favorite musicians is Bob Dylan, and he wrote a famous song called "Blowin' in the Wind." Like alotta songs, it is basically poetry set to music. Anyway, it's about being frustrated and fed up with war. There's one part that kind of says it all. It goes like this:

> *Yes, 'n' how many times must the cannon balls fly Before they're forever banned?*

My dad says this song helped bring people together because it was able to say what millions of people felt. At peace rallies, people started to sing this song together. And it became an anthem for the antiwar movement of the 1960s. It was a poem that helped change the world.

So pick something in your life or in the world that's not quite as great as you'd like it to be. It might be how you get along with one of your friends or family. It might be something in your school or in your house, or something you read about on the Internet, in a newspaper, in a magazine, or whatever. Think about how you'd like to change this thing. Now write your poem. You can even rhyme if you're so inclined.

_____

_____

_____

_____

_____

_____

_____

_____

_____

_____

ACTIVITY 5:
Do the Haiku

One of the oldest kinds of poetry is the haiku. It's originally Japanese, but anybody can do it. The thing that makes haiku hard is also what makes it wickedly excellent: the very strict rules. First of all, every haiku should only have three lines. Second of all, each line should only have a certain number of syllables. Here's the deal:

> *Line 1: 5 syllables*
> *Line 2: 7 syllables*
> *Line 3: 5 syllables*

Haiku used to be only about nature—you know, like trees and frogs and tree frogs. And alotta times haiku would be set in a season, like summer, or spring, or whatever. Now people write about all kinds of things in their haiku—eating, shopping, washing the dishes. Personally, I like to

The Writer in Me **33**

snap crackle pop!

Here's a list I came up with recently that helped me write a haiku: *electric bass, snowflake, Rice Krispies, paintbrush, old goat, beaded lamp, big fish, polka-dot socks, milk, boogers, ostrich, camera, pig, spider web.* **And here's the haiku I ended up with:**

Crispy Haiku

Rice Krispies in bowl
Carefully pour in white milk
Wow! Snap crackle pop.

make sure I follow the rules, even if I don't write about nature or a season. It's kinda like when you write 5–7–5, it forces you to really boil something down to exactly what it is, because you have only a tiny number of words to do the whole thing. Ready to haiku?

First, you gotta make some super lists:

- ❁ Make a list of things in nature.
- ❁ Make a list of things around you.
- ✳ Make a list of things you love.
- ❁ Make a list of things you hate.
- ❁ Make a list of random things, whatever lands in your mind.

Now pick some things from your list, and start playing with the words. Arrange them and rearrange them on the page. Count the syllables. Put them together in all different ways, until they fit perfectly into a 5–7–5 haiku.

chapter three:
the playwright
in me

When I was a little kid, my dad took me to the musical *The Lion King*. First we saw the movie, which I thought was pretty decent, but the play was ten billion times better. The costumes made my eyes almost pop outta my head, and I couldn't believe how much the dancers made the gazelle, hyena, and lion puppets move like real animals. I can honestly say I've never seen a play like it in my entire life.

Before the show, when the lights went out, everyone sat completely silent, waiting for the play to start. It was so exciting, I actually got little goose bumps (hey, why do they call them goose bumps anyway? They don't look like geese!). Ever since then, I've been writing plays and putting them on with my friends.

"I'd like to do a play more than anything. First night is the most exciting thing in the world. It's wonderful to hear your words spoken." —Dorothy Parker, Writer

Last year, my dad built a cool stage under the big old tree in our front yard, and we did our performances there. We even started charging money for tickets!

People have been putting on plays for thousands of years, and alotta these totally old plays still get put on today. The ancient Greeks and Romans (I'm talking from 500 to 400 B.C. here) performed the first plays, like *Oedipus Rex* and *The Frogs*. And for centuries now, plays have been put on in big cities like Paris, London, and New York (where Broadway is). Actually, alotta the most famous plays in the world, like William Shakespeare's *The Tempest*, were originally written and performed for kings and queens and their courts. No lowly peons like you or me allowed!

There's also been a long history of troupes of actors who would travel to towns to put on plays. The play would be a majorly major event, and nearly everyone would come watch. Kinda like when everyone goes out to see the first night of a blockbuster movie—only if you missed the first night, you couldn't go any other day that week. You'd have to wait until the next time the troupe rolled into town—and that could be a whole year later!

Whether old or new, plays come in all shapes and sizes: tragedies, dramas, short plays, long plays, and kooky plays that don't make any sense (those are called absurd plays). And let's not forget musicals, one of my ATFs! Behind each of these plays is a playwright, a genius like you or me—the brains (and pen) behind the action.

So far, I've written four plays. One is a comedy called *My Mom Is a Spy,* which I mentioned before. It's about what seems like an uber-normal family, only

didya know?!

the mom is a secret agent, and nobody knows it. But by the end, everyone in the family figures it all out because they begin spying on the mom! My musical *The Playground* is about a bunch of bullies and the kids they pick on. It started as a poem, kinda like "hard in the schoolyard," then morphed into a spoken-word musical. I also wrote a tragedy, *The Day My Dog Died.* I don't think I need to tell you what that's about (sniff, sniff). And my other play is absurd. Too absurd to talk about now—I'll tell you more a little later.

In fact, I'm gonna tell you about how to write lots of different kinds of plays. So, let the lights fade, the curtain rise, and the playwriting begin!

ACTIVITY 1:

On the Edge of Your Seat

One of my favorite plays is *The Odd Couple* by Neil Simon. It's about two roommates —one is a really neat perfectionist and the other is a big slob who throws his stuff all over the place. The neatnik character, Felix, is always trying to convince the messy character, Oscar, to clean up his act; and at the same time, Oscar is always trying to convince Felix to be a more happy-go-lucky, free-to-be-you-and-me kinda guy. So you can imagine how annoyed they get at each other.

So one night, Felix makes a special linguini dish for dinner. During the meal, Oscar calls the linguini "spaghetti." Felix turns to Oscar and snaps in a snobby and snippy way, "It's not spaghetti, it's linguini." Oscar picks up the plate of food and throws it against the wall, where it explodes in a horrible mess. Then he turns to Felix and says, "Now, it's garbage!"

While you watch this scene, you can't help but ask, "Will they stay friends?! Will they kill each other?! What's gonna happen next?!" That's because there's so much "dramatic tension." Dramatic tension is when, you know, everything is all tense and dramatic. It's when the whole audience feels excited and on the edge of their seats.

Every play has to have lots of dramatic tension. Otherwise, people will get bored and start counting the white hairs on the head of the old guy sitting in front of them. Here's a great way to practice creating dramatic tension: Write a scene where one person is trying to convince someone else to do something. Anything. Whatever. Could be to make a bet, pay a debt, or take their cat to the vet. Play around with making the characters really different from each other. Maybe one character talks in really long run-on sentences, and the other only says "yes" or "no." Maybe one is totally emotional and the other person never reveals what she really feels. Maybe one is way allergic to cats while the other keeps petting the cat in the room and blowing the cat hair all over the place. Here's the conversation I hear in my head for that specific situation:

Person Allergic to Cats
(really angry)
I can't stand it one more minute! Not one more second! Who do you think you are, petting that cat while I'm sitting here sneezing, sneezing, coughing, wheezing?! I'm telling you to get rid of that darn cat or something really, really, really bad will happen!

Cat Lover
(with no emotion)
No.

Person Allergic to Cats
(about to blow a fuse)
If you don't get rid of the cat, I'm going to take the kitty litter and put it all over the carpet in your room! In fact, I'm going to put it on your bed!! No, on your pillowcase!!!

Cat Lover
(with no emotion)
I don't care.

What dialogue is brewing in your head? Is it getting tense in there? Write it down!

_____

_____

_____

_____

_____

_____

_____

_____

_____

_____

ACTIVITY 2:

What a Character!

One of the hardest things to do is to create a character that seems really real, but is also amazingly interesting. One way to learn how is to take characters that are already out there, ones that somebody else made up or ones that you know really well, and put them into new and interesting situations.

So pick two of your favorite characters from a TV show, play, movie, or book. Write a scene between the two of them. You can choose two characters from the same TV show, movie, play, or book, or from completely different ones. Like have Alice (of *Alice in Wonderland* fame) go shopping for a pair of her own red ruby slippers with Dorothy (from *The Wonderful Wizard of Oz*). Or maybe Nancy Drew and Lisa Simpson chug up Mount Everest

together. Think about how the characters talk, whether they like pasta or pizza, and whether they show their feelings or keep them all bottled up. When you put two characters together, you'll start noticing what makes them special.

_____
_____
_____
_____
_____
_____
_____
_____
_____
_____
_____
_____
_____
_____
_____
_____
_____
_____
_____

ACTIVITY 3:
Sing the Thing

I don't know a single person who doesn't love music. Maybe that's because a really good song can make you wanna jump outta your seat and boogie, or can calm you down when you feel like exploding. . . . Whatever the reason, it's probably why so many people go gaga over musicals. Me included. One of my favorite musicals is *Guys and Dolls*. There's this great scene where all these old-school, gangster-type guys sing a song called "Sit Down, You're Rockin' the Boat" in this crazy harmony. I tell ya, when I saw it live, I could actually feel the music vibrating through my whole body—in my heart, my muscles, even in my bones. It was one of the coolest things ever.

Musicals are usually written by two people—a lyricist (who writes the words to the song) and a composer (who writes the

The Writer in Me **41**

absurdly absurd

If comedies, tragedies, or even musicals aren't your thing, why not try a kind of play that jumps right out of the box? In the Theater of the Absurd, plays don't make sense on purpose. This kind of play was popular from the 1940s to the 1960s and supposedly came out of the nonsense poetry of the Dadaists (a cool group of artists from the early twentieth century). When I found out about it, I thought, "What a cool idea!" Topsy-turvy plots, kooky characters, and dialogue that repeats itself, and dialogue that repeats itself, and dialogue that repeats itself—just my kinda thing!

My absurd play is called *Two Heads Are Better Than One*. It's about one person who has two heads. Jasmine and I have put it on a few times. We climb into a big zip-up, one-piece snowsuit thing, so it looks like we're one person with two heads. But Jasmine's half of the costume is polka dots and my half is stripes. So then we start yelling these bizarro facts at each other. Stuff like, "The average life of a mosquito is *X* days!" And, "When you breed a cocker spaniel and a poodle you get a cockapoo!"

We scream this stuff like we're really, really, mad, and our faces get all red, and spit flies everywhere. Then Jasmine starts yelling "Polka dots!" and I start yelling "Stripes!" We get in a crazy play-fight and start rolling around on the floor like a couple of lunatics stuffed in a jumpsuit. Then I accidentally switch to screaming "Polka dots!" and Jasmine switches to "Stripes!" Suddenly, we stop, look at each other, and bust out laughing.

Go ahead, and try to write an absurd play crazier than that! It helps to think of it like a Mad Lib: Choose the wackiest characters you can think of, the randomest plot, and the most ridiculous lines. Then throw 'em all in a pot, turn up the heat, and stir until you've got an absolutely fabulously absurd play.

music). Sometimes, the words will be written first, sometimes the melody. Like one of my favorite songs from a musical is "Sunrise, Sunset," from *Fiddler on the Roof*. I always thought that the words must have been written before the music because they're just so perfect and sad, sad, sad (if you ever have the chance to see *Fiddler* in a theater, take a look around you during this song and you'll see lots of people crying).

But it turns out that the music was written first. The interesting thing is that the lyricist said he could just hear the lyrics as the music played. So, sometimes the words inspire the music and sometimes it's the opposite. In addition to the lyricist and composer, there's often a third person who helps write a musical. This person writes what's called "the book"—that's all the lines of dialogue that are not set to music.

So as you can see, there's a lot that goes on in a musical! So how do you even know where to start? Some musicals are based on a story that already exists. Like Stephen Sondheim and Leonard Bernstein took *Romeo and Juliet,* set it in a different time and place, and turned it into a musical called *West Side Story*. Or sometimes a musical is born outta history or an important person, like *Jesus Christ Superstar*. But no matter what, in really good musicals, the songs help tell the story.

Because the sound of music can be so inspiring and because it can be really hard to write a song from scratch (especially if you're not so musically inclined), here's a cool way of learning how to become a master lyricist: Take a song from one of your favorite musicals and rewrite the words to fit the musical *you* have in mind. In fact, you can write an entire musical using other people's songs—just change the words. You can also use regular old music, too: pop, oldies, folk, country, whatever. The point is to figure out how to write your own words to music. And to actually tell a story while the music plays on.

ACTIVITY 4:
Silence Is Golden

A lotta people think that plays are just actors yakking or singing to each other. But so much important stuff can happen in a play without any dialogue—slumped shoulders, a frown, stabbing someone in the heart with a dagger—you get the idea. Actions sometimes actually do speak louder than words. It's just like real life. If someone looks at you in just the right way, she can make you laugh, or make you mad, sad, confused, or whatever.

Like the other day, my room was a total, total, total, total, total, total, total mess. Even for me. So my mom walked in, and she just stared at me. She didn't say one single word, but I could tell she was so crazy mad at me. I could practically see little knives coming outta her eyes. Then she turned around and stormed out.

Well, believe me, I knew exactly how upset she was, and if we had been onstage, I guarantee you that the audience would have known, too. Needless to say, I cleaned up my room lickety-split.

Now, think about the power of my mom's glare and write a scene where two characters don't say anything out loud at all. Not one single word. Zilch, zero, nada, nothing. Choose an activity—cooking a midnight feast, opening presents, even cleaning your room—and build a story around it using actions and expressions only. Think hard about the

didya know?!

How do you write a silent scene? Through what are called "stage directions." If you have ever read a play, you know what I'm talking about: They're instructions from the playwright about how actors should come onto stage, move, and behave, as well as notes about what should happen with lights, props, or the set. Things like, "Stage right, the Princess tosses and turns on a pile of five mattresses. She throws her arms up in distress—no matter how hard she tries, she cannot get to sleep." Or, "The lights dim, and the Giant Hamster creeps onto stage as the vampire falls asleep, curled on his side." So if you're writing a scene without any dialogue, you're obviously going to need alotta stage directions. This way, your actors won't just sit on the stage like blobs, but will flow through scenes seamlessly as they tell your whole story without a single word!

emotions you want each person to show and what movements each actor needs to make (or not make) to show it. How much can you have the actor say without talking?

_____

_____

_____

_____

_____

_____

_____

_____

_____

_____

_____

_____

_____

_____

_____

_____

_____

_____

_____

ACTIVITY 5:
Getting to Know Your Characters

A good way to get to know the characters in your play is to write mini-scenes where they react to different situations that do NOT happen in your play at all. Let's say you're writing a play about a super-shy girl who's starting school in a new city, and all the action takes place during her first day of class. Try writing these scenes with your character in mind. What happens? Remember, none of it will end up in your play, but it'll help you understand who your character really is.

✳ Write a scene (scene 1) in which your character gets yelled at by her older brother when she first wakes up in the morning. What does she do? Does she yell back at him? Does she tell her mom? Does she throw a tantrum? Or does she take it out on her annoying little sister?

❇ Write a scene (scene 2) in which your character gets lost in a train station and has to ask strangers for help. How does she react? Does she sit down and take a deep breath? Does she cry? Or is she scared but trying not to show it?

❇ Write a scene (scene 3) in which your character finds out she just won two million dollars, and she's home alone except for her dog, Snickerdoodle. Does she jump and scream? Does she hug Snickerdoodle? Or does she get bummed that she's always alone when good things happen?

Now use the information you gathered. Like, if your character's the type who cries at the train station, maybe she slips into the bathroom to cry at lunch because she's so nervous. Or if she's the type who celebrates with her dog, maybe she befriends a ladybug in the schoolyard. Once you've thought about this stuff, give the play itself a whirl. It'll be a lot easier to write since you know your character so well now.

Scene 1

_____
_____
_____
_____
_____
_____
_____
_____
_____
_____
_____
_____
_____
_____
_____
_____
_____
_____
_____

Scene 2

_____
_____
_____
_____
_____
_____
_____
_____
_____
_____
_____
_____
_____
_____
_____
_____
_____
_____
_____
_____
_____
_____
_____
_____
_____
_____

Scene 3

_____
_____
_____
_____
_____
_____
_____
_____
_____
_____
_____
_____
_____
_____
_____
_____
_____
_____
_____
_____
_____
_____
_____
_____
_____

chapter four:

the
screenwriter
in me

It used to be that the only people who could make movies had tons of money and expensive cameras. Now you can make a movie with a PHONE! Look at me, I've personally made five movies. Well, actually four and a half—I haven't quite finished the last one because my inflatable globe popped while we were shooting a scene, and I've been so slammed lately that I haven't had a chance to get a new one.

It's a sci-fi movie called *The MissMatched Planet That Time Forgot,* and I can't wait to finish it.

But I'm getting ahead of myself. Let's go back in time a bit. The first movies, made in the nineteenth century, were black and white, didn't have any sound, and didn't even have stories. Sounds entertaining, right? It wasn't until around 1900 that people started adding a story to what were called "moving pictures" (that's where the word "movie" comes from, in case you wondered). Because the movies were silent, all the dialogue was

didya know?!

Sometimes in Hollywood, screenplays get sick. Like if a script for a comedy isn't funny enough, or a thriller isn't thrilling, or a tearjerker doesn't jerk enough tears, a Hollywood studio will bring in a "script doctor" to fix whatever's wrong with it. A script doctor can work for a week or for a year. And sometimes, when a screenplay is really sick, like on its deathbed, it needs a whole team of doctors to make it all better!

written on cards and filmed with a camera so that the audience could read the words. To make it more fun to go to the movies, theaters would hire a pianist or organist to play music while the movie ran.

So, when you wrote a screenplay in the old days, it was all about lots of action with as little dialogue as possible. All that changed in the 1920s when inventors figured out how to add sound to movies. And these films were called "talkies," for pretty obvious reasons!

If you wanna make a good movie (or talkie!), it really helps to write a good screenplay. And one of the cool things about a screenplay is that you can write it and then let someone else turn it into a movie if you don't feel like doing it yourself. But I gotta tell ya, half the fun of writing a screenplay is bringing it to life on camera. Cuz sometimes the best person to make your movie happen is you.

But back to writing! One of my dad's friends is a screenwriter. Recently, he showed me some of his stuff. The first screenplay was mad long—over 100 pages. But he also showed me a couple of short screenplays that he wrote. One was only a page long! And after he explained the whole idea to me, I was like, "Hey, I could completely write a one-page script." So I did! And that was my first movie: *Sock Monkeys Gone Wrong*. I had crazy fun writing it. Then Jasmine and I shot it on my dad's camcorder. Afterward, we downloaded it onto my computer and put credits on it and everything. You know, like:

Starring
LittleMissMatched

Directed by
Jasmine

Edited by
Dad

Then we burned it onto a DVD and gave it out to all our friends. Everyone liked it a lot, and then a couple of my amigas made their own movies. Some of them were really, really good.

But no matter what kind of movie you wanna make, like I said, the first thing to do is actually write a screenplay. A screenplay is different from a book, because in a screenplay all you have is what you see and what you hear. That's it! Eyes and ears. In a short story or a poem or whatever, you can describe a lot more stuff, like how people feel and what they're like and where they're from.

But it's kinda cool, actually, to see how much of a story you can tell just using pictures and sounds and how you end up working in feelings and thoughts in other ways. Hopefully that's what the activities that follow will help you do. So get your screenwriter's pen out and let your mind go wild. Before you know it you'll be yelling, "Lights! Camera! Action!"

ACTIVITY 1:

Be the Camera

If you wanna write a movie, you should try to look at the world like you're a camera. It's easy, too. All you have to do is to make your hands into the frame of a camera. Put your hands together with the tips of your thumbs touching each other and your index fingers pointing straight up toward the sky (like in the picture above). Move your hands left and right, toward your eyes and away from them. It's like you're seeing the world through the same rectangle as you would with a movie camera.

When you look at the world through your hand camera, you really do see it in a different way. It helps you focus on what the person watching your movie will actually see, like the stuff in the room and the way people are acting. So when you walk into a room, use your hand camera to zoom in on the tiniest things. Then zoom out to the biggest.

Like, when you go over to your friend's house, really, really look at what's in her room. What does it say about a person when her room is a big mess? Or when everything's so super-neat it looks like the whole room is being strangled into order? What books are on the shelves? What posters hang on the walls?

Pick an object that shows the mood that you want your movie to have. Now use your hands to figure out what part of that object to focus on so that your audience will get your point. Like I wanted to use Jasmine's really gorgeous kimono for a movie. So, I used my hand camera to look at the

> **"An actor entering through the door; you've got nothing. But if he enters through the window, you've got a situation."**
> —Billy Wilder, Screenwriter and Filmmaker

kimono really close, and it was pretty amazing, actually.

I mean I've looked at this kimono a billion times, but when I saw it through my hand camera, I noticed how beautiful the dragon that curls around the back is. And when I moved my hand camera, I realized that right next to the dragon was an awesome lady I had never seen before. So I decided to start my movie off by focusing on the dragon. Then I'd move to the lady, and then to Jasmine's face, which would be covered in white makeup, with painted red lips—all while mad cool Japanese music plays in the background. I thought this would be uber-artistic. I don't know whether it will work or not on screen, but it sure looked infinitely interesting when I saw it through my hand camera. And the great thing about the technique is that you can use your hand camera anywhere. At school, in the car, in the bathroom, at the mall, you name it!

But enough talk. It's time to put your hand camera to work. Now, use your trusty new device to examine a location where you wanna film your movie. Choose five interesting things in it and describe what each item tells you about this place, the person who lives there, or the overall idea of your movie.

Location

Item 1: _____
What it says: _____
_____

Item 2: _____
What it says: _____
_____

Item 3: _____
What it says: _____
_____

Item 4: _____
What it says: _____
_____

Item 5: _____
What it says: _____
_____

Now use your hand camera to look at people. Check out people's body language. Notice how much they say with their bodies, even when they're not moving their mouths. Like when someone keeps tapping his foot, usually it means he's nervous, or feeling kinda tweaky. Or if someone blinks a lot, maybe that's because she has something to hide. Sometimes people say one thing with their bodies and a totally different thing with their mouths. Like my sister might tell my mother that she did her homework, but her eyes will go all shifty and she'll swallow extra hard, because she's actually telling a big fat fib. Later you can use your real camera to catch stuff like that.

So use your hand camera to watch people move. Then describe five cool movements or gestures in the fill-in section below:

People

Movement 1: _____
_____
_____

Movement 2: _____
_____
_____

Movement 3: _____
_____
_____

Movement 4: _____
_____
_____

Movement 5: _____
_____
_____

LMM tip

It's fun to see what things look like really, really close up. You can even start one of your scenes with the camera so close to something that you can't quite make out what it is. And then when you pull the camera back, your audience will totally recognize what they were looking at.

Like in my vampire movie, *Kiss of the Krazy Kitty,* I started out with a close-up of Chile Pepper, my movie-star cat. It looked really cool, but you couldn't quite tell what it was. And then the further the camera moved back, the more you could recognize it was a cat's eye. Everybody who saw the scene thought it was really awesome. I came up with the idea one day when I got really close to Chile Pepper's eye. I saw how incredibly excellent it looked, like you could kind of see through it, but you kind of couldn't, all at the same time.

ACTIVITY 2:
Characters, Locations, Props & More!

When you wanna write a screenplay, you need to figure out some key details:

❋ What kinda people, or characters, you're gonna write about.

❋ Where you want all the action to take place, or what location you wanna use.

❋ What kinda stuff, or props, you wanna put in your story.

That's why, especially if it's a screenplay I plan to make into a movie myself, I like to make lists of characters, locations, and props before I even think about exactly what the story is gonna be about. Cuz, let's say you wanna do a movie that takes place by the ocean, but you live in the middle of the mountains. You're gonna have a serious situation on your hands. Point is, you really gotta think things out first. Filling in the following lists will help you get started.

Characters:

These people (or animals, for that matter) could be in my movie:

Character 1: _____
_____
_____

Character 2: _____
_____
_____

Character 3: _____
_____
_____

Character 4: _____
_____
_____

Character 5: _____
_____
_____

Locations:

My movie could take place here:

Location 1: _____
_____
_____
_____

Location 2: _____
_____
_____

Location 3: _____
_____
_____

Location 4: _____
_____
_____

Location 5: _____
_____
_____

LMM list

Characters

Chile Pepper (of course), Jasmine, Grandpa, Mr. Moore from the candy store, my sister (if I can bribe her into it)

Settings

My room, Jasmine's garage, the park near my mom's office, the zoo, the cool Chinese restaurant downtown with all the paper lanterns

Props

Grandpa's Winnebago, Jasmine's kimono, my bass guitar, an inflatable globe with a hole in it, my dad's golf clubs, 134 mismatched socks

Props:

I could use this stuff in my movie:

Prop 1: _____

_____

_____

Prop 2: _____

_____

Prop 3: _____

_____

Prop 4: _____

_____

Prop 5: _____

_____

_____

Okay, now take a look at your locations, characters, and props. Start mixing and matching people with places, places with things, and things with people. Is a story starting to bubble in your head?

Don't worry if your idea seems lame at first. Think more about it and discuss it with friends. Try writing about it here. You never know what kinda wild and crazy story it could grow into.

ACTIVITY 3:

Didya Hear That?!

DRIP
DRIP
DRIP

Okay, think for a sec about the kind of things you hear in a movie. First of all, there's the stuff you hear in the background, like a baby crying, or an airplane flying by, or maybe a faucet dripping. Then there's the stuff people say to each other—the dialogue. You might also hear a "voice-over." That's when you record somebody talking, and then run the sound over the action. So you don't actually see the person speaking, but you hear him or her talking about the story in general, while you watch something else.

Filmmakers can also use music to create a most excellent mood. It's amazing how a soundtrack can make a scene seem mad happy, or totally tense, or crazy scary. Next time you watch a movie, listen really hard to the music. You'll be shocked by how much of a difference it makes. Like one time when I was channel surfing, I found this movie with a scene where this warbly little kids' song, like a lullaby, was playing on a tinkly little piano. It was really creepy! I was so freaked out that I put the TV on mute, and what happened was pretty crazy—without the sound, the movie wasn't scary at all. It was just a shot of a boring, dark room. When I un-muted, I got creeped out all over again, just cuz of the music!

So, while you're thinking about the people, places, and stuff you want in your screenplay, also start to think about what you wanna hear. Start with background music and make a playlist for your film using the chart on the next page.

My Movie Playlist	
Scene	**Song**
Opener *(plays over credits)*	
Scene 1	
Scene 2	
Scene 3	
Scene 4	
Closer *(last song heard)*	

Next, figure out what background sounds you wanna hear. Should birds be chirping outside when things are happy? A clock ticking or a heart beating when something totally spooky is happening? Wind blowing in a scene where the characters are scared outta their wits?

Write down any sound notes in the chart on the next page. It has two categories, character and location, so you can keep better track of who and what your sounds match up with. Like, if your character is taking an important test but can't think of an answer, you could write "pencil tapping" under "character" and "lights buzzing" under "location."

My Movie Sound List		
Scene	Character	Location
Opener		
Scene 1		
Scene 2		
Scene 3		
Scene 4		
Closer		

ACTIVITY 4:

Monkey See, Monkey Do

One of the best ways to learn how to write a good screenplay is to watch lots of great movies. Cuddle up on the couch with your favorite DVD or head over to the local theater and take it all in with a big carton of popcorn. Study what the camera focuses on, what the characters are wearing, how they move their bodies, the ways they talk to each other, the background sounds, the music, and the way the story is told. Whether it's a comedy, a drama, a musical, a documentary, or anything in between, you can always learn something by watching a movie that's totally, awesomely excellent.

Start by making a list of your favorite movies:

1. _____

2. _____

3. _____

4. _____

5. _____

6. _____

7. _____

8. _____

9. _____

10. _____

Now write down exactly what you love about these movies in the space to the right. Is there a character who only has one line, but who totally cracks you up? Or is there a costume that is the most beautiful thing you've ever seen? Is there a piece of music that makes you cry when you hear it in a particular scene? After you've collected your favorite things, you can use them as ideas for your own screenplays. Obviously, you don't wanna copy them completely, but lots of filmmakers do take actual shots from their most-loved movies and re-create them in their own unique way.

_____
_____
_____
_____
_____
_____
_____
_____
_____
_____
_____
_____
_____

mad cool movies

Here are some of my ATF movies:

Charlotte's Web

The Wizard of Oz

Clueless

Happy Feet

Mad Hot Ballroom

National Velvet

Akeela and the Bee

West Side Story

The Incredibles

The Sound of Music

The Little Mermaid

The Princess Bride

Some Like It Hot

The Parent Trap

ACTIVITY 5:
The Nuts and Bolts of the Screenplay

The way a screenplay is written on a page looks totally different from a short story or a novel, but it's not too different from a play. Like when you start a scene, the very first thing you have to write down is the location. Then in the next line, you have to describe what the camera shows, and if there are any noises or sounds. Plus, if you want music playing in the background, you have to include that, too.

Here's an example from one of my screenplays. It's actually pretty straightforward, and once you get the hang of the format, writing becomes a whole lot easier. (If you don't know what something means, check out my definitions of words and abbreviations on page 67.)

The Case of the Missing Mouse

by LittleMissMatched

INT. Totally messy room, midday. CLOSE-UP of CHILE PEPPER walking straight toward us, looking as cool as a cat, with a small head and huge eyes, big ears, and long whiskers. She's black and white, and has two mismatched socks for paws. "Stray Cat Shuffle," by the Stray Cats, plays in the background. She walks through a giant mess: dirty laundry, old shoes, crayons, stuffed dogs and cats and giraffes, books, CDs, DVDs, old juice containers, and mismatched socks strewn everywhere.

Then if you wanna have people talking to each other, you have to:

* Announce the name of the character who's talking.

* Say the way in which he or she is going to act out the line.

* Write what the character says. Like this:

Mom
(*Ticked off*)
I thought I told you to clean up this room?! I've never seen such a pigsty! In fact, a pig would be embarrassed to be in this room!

LittleMissMatched
(*Sassy*)
Really? I think a pig would LOVE my room!

If you want a voice-over, you just write the name of the character who's talking, and then next to that you write V.O. in parentheses. Then on the next line you write the voice-over itself, like this:

Chile Pepper (V.O.)
(*Excited*)
Oooooh! Dirty laundry!!! My favorite thing to curl up in!

I know it sounds kinda confusing, but once you get the

hang of it, you'll see it's not that hard. Like I said, if I can do it, you can, too. Try out the fill-ins below to get the hang of what I'm talking about. Then start screenwriting!

Location [INT. or EXT.?]:

_____

_____

What does the camera see?:

_____

_____

What do you hear? Music? Sounds?:

_____

_____

Name of character:

_____

_____

Character's attitude:
[V.O. or No V.O.?]

_____

_____

Dialogue:

_____

the movie skinny

Here are some words and abbreviations you'll need to know to write a real Hollywood screenplay:

Close-up: What you see when the camera zooms in on something and gets really, really close.

Credits: A list of all the people who worked on the movie, like the director, the screenwriter, the editor, the caterer who makes and brings the sandwiches (if you're lucky enough to have someone bring you food while you work!), and everybody and anybody else you wanna thank. The credits go at the end of the movie, and usually it's good to have some totally wicked music playing over them.

Dialogue: Words the characters say.

EXT.: Exterior (that's outside, duh!).

INT.: Interior (that's inside, double duh!).

Location: Where the action is taking place.

Pan: To move your camera side-to-side or up and down to show your audience the big picture. Like in *The Wonderful Wizard of Oz,* when Dorothy lands, the camera pans so we can see the whole wacky wonderful world of Munchkinland.

Point of View: Whose eyes we're seeing the action through.

Voice-over: A recorded speech or narration that is then played over the action.

Zoom: To make the camera move either closer to the action or further away. Most cameras have a "Zoom" button. When you push on one side of the button, you get closer to the action, and when you push the other side, you move further and further away.

chapter five:

the journal writer in me

D o you remember Beatrix Potter? She's the author of the Peter Rabbit books that you may have read when you were little. You know, the naughty rabbit that escapes from Mr. McGregor's garden. Well, it turns out that Beatrix loved to write in her journal. She was a bit on the shy side, so she liked to take notes on people, places, animals, and all kinds of other things in nature. She would imitate people's accents in her journal or note down cool-sounding sounds like "lippity, lippity." And sometimes she would write stuff about people that they might not be that excited to hear (if you know what I mean). Maybe that's why parts of her journal were written in a secret code. That's right, a secret code!

Beatrix also used her secret code to write about how disappointed she was that her scientific theories were not taken seriously. See, Beatrix used her journals to make all kinds of observations about nature that people had not made before. But because she lived during a time when women weren't allowed in scientific societies, it was very hard to get professional scientists to listen to her ideas. In fact, Beatrix wasn't even allowed to present her own ideas at scientific meetings—she had to have a man do it for her! The good news is that, later, her journals helped show that she was a totally top biological thinker of her time. Not to mention a really great writer and illustrator who had a super-awesome sense of humor!

Like Beatrix, I love my journal. I carry it with me wherever I go. I even have different-sized journals. Like if I'm going somewhere and I don't have my backpack, I take a little travel journal along for the ride (one comes with the kit). It fits right inside my pocket. See, the thing is, you never know when you're gonna get a most excellent idea, or hear some crazy thing somebody says, or read something that's super-interesting. But if

you've got your journal with you, you can break it out and write it down!

Plus, when you have your journal, you can escape into your own little world, no matter where you are—on the bus, in a car, or even if you have to eat at a truly heinous restaurant with a bunch of people you don't know, just cuz it's good for your mom's business. All I have to do is whip out my journal, and I can go wherever I wanna go, be whomever I wanna be.

I love to write down whole conversations in my journal. Like one time, I wrote down exactly what my sister said when she had a total temper tantrum— she just completely lost her mind!

LMM tip

Sometimes I also like to tape or glue stuff into my journal—pictures, mementos, souvenirs. Like if I find a feather somewhere, or a ticket stub for a movie I saw, or maybe if someone sent me a card, I might paste it in there. That way my journal also becomes a scrapbook. That's the crazy cool thing about a journal: It's whatever you want it to be!

And then I read it to my best friend, and we nearly peed in our pants, it was so funny. This may sound like a ridiculous thing to do. But as I said before, it'll actually make you a better writer cuz you'll learn how to write the way people *really* talk.

Once I read about a study where scientists had people write down the most totally heinous stuff that ever happened to them. Then the scientists tested everybody and found out that the people's immune systems (that's what stops you from getting sick) got better and stronger and more excellent after they wrote this stuff down. I couldn't believe it! They weren't taking vitamin C, or eating chicken soup, or anything. Just writing stuff down.

Ever since I heard that, I've been writing down every single horrible thing that ever happened to me, even if it was only a tiny smidge horrible. Like one time I was at the beach, and I took my shoes and socks off, and rolled my pants up, and walked right in the ocean. I loved the feeling of the waves going in and out over my legs and my toes when I gripped the sand.

But when I came back out, I saw that I had put my socks too close to the water. This massive, gnarly wave had dragged them out to sea! I just had to watch my socks as they got tinier and tinier until, finally, they just disappeared. And they were my ATF socks! One of them had turquoise dolphins on it, and the other one had moss-green whales. The whole thing ruined my day at the beach and I turned into a massive sulky pill. Man, I loved those socks.

On the way home in the car, I got out my journal and started to write about it. And I had a picture in my head of my two favorite socks getting dragged down to the bottom of the sea—where they lived in a hundred-tentacled octopus's garden with nutty lobsters, hammerhead sharks, seahorses, and sea anemones. After I wrote all the stuff down, I felt relieved. I realized those scientists were right—writing does make you feel sooooooo much better!

Journaling is also a great way to keep track of your life. You can look back later and remember all the stuff you did. I love reading my old journals and thinking about what I was going through at school, or with my friends, or on summer vacation. Alotta the stuff

I had totally forgotten about. It's almost like reading a book about your own life. Plus, whenever I'm confused about something, or stuff doesn't make sense, I write about it in my journal—afterward, I almost always understand it better. Or when I'm mad at somebody, I write about it. And alotta times I realize I was mad about something else.

Your journal is a place you can be totally yourself. Say anything you want about anybody or whatever. Your dreams, your nightmares, your hopes, your fears, when you're totally happy or when you're mad sad. Things you can't tell anybody else, you can tell to your journal. The most important things, and the silliest stuff. Later, you can use the things in your journal to help you write plays, screenplays, stories, poems, whatever. And, as everyone knows, the more you write, the better writer you'll become.

The Writer in Me **71**

Write What You Know, Know How to Write

I read in a book somewhere that you should write about what you know. Your memories are a great place to start. Good ones, bad ones, funny ones, sad ones, old ones, crazy ones.

Write your earliest memory down. Now write down everything else you could possibly remember about it. How old were you? What were you wearing? What did your hair look like? What were you thinking? What were you feeling? Who else was there? What were they doing? The more details the better.

Keep writing down your memories. Make an ongoing list of them in your journal. Work your way down the list, answering all the questions above. It will help you learn about yourself, and it will help you learn to describe things in a way that will make people say, "I know *exactly* what you're talking about!"

Like one time I was remembering my first day of middle school. How I'd convinced myself that I'd worn a really dorky sweatshirt and how I hid during lunch so that I wouldn't have to figure out who to sit next to. After I wrote all about it in my journal, I used it to write a short story called "Uncool at School." When I read it during English class, kids said they totally related to it, cuz they had all felt the same way at some point, even though they thought nobody else did.

_____

_____

_____

_____

_____

_____

_____

LMM tip

Has someone done something really terrible to you? Does it swirl around in your memory and make your mad meter go off the charts? Here's a fun and helpful thing to do: Write a letter to this person—one that you don't send. Like, last year, I had five dollars hidden in my drawer, and then it suddenly disappeared. I just knew my sister took it. So I wrote a crazy mad, furious letter where I called her every horrible name I knew. Plus a few I made up. But I didn't give her the letter. I just used the space to vent. Well it turns out, I—my very own self—had moved the money and forgotten about it. You can imagine how glad I was I didn't send that letter! But I did get some excellent material for a screenplay I was writing about two sisters who get in a bad fight!!!

ACTIVITY 2:

The Where of There

No matter what you're writing, if you can make whoever's reading it feel like they're actually there, in the story, then you've done a most excellent job. A good way to do this is to really pay attention to what's around you.

Like, one time I was waiting for the bus, and I saw a woman feeding the pigeons under the glass bus shelter. She had big, thick hands, and big, thick legs, but a tiny little head. And the more she fed the pigeons, the more pigeons showed up, until hundreds of pigeons surrounded her, clustered in this glass box. The flap-flapping of their wings gave me the creeps. But I couldn't erase the scene from my mind. So I wrote about it in my journal. I handed it in as an assignment for my English class, and my teacher, Ms. Radcliffe, told me it was one of her favorite things I ever wrote. She said she could see and hear exactly what was happening at the bus stop—like she was watching it on the screen in a movie theater.

As you go through your day, pick five different places to write about. A special place. A boring place. A familiar place. An exciting place. Or whatever kind of place you happen to be in when you pull out your journal. Describe it from up close and from far away. What colors do you see? What does it smell like? Is anything moving, or is everything still? Are there people around? Are there noises? Use all this stuff to make the place come alive in your journal.

didya know?!

A journal can be like a diary, where you write down stuff that happens to you every day. One of the most famous diaries was written by Anne Frank, a Jewish girl who hid from the Nazis in an attic in Amsterdam with her family.

Anne had been given a diary for her thirteenth birthday, and she used it to write down the details of what happened to her during this horrible time. She wrote all about her family and what was going on with them. She recorded the day-to-day stuff, like what they talked about at dinner, or when she had an argument with her mom. But she also wrote about bigger stuff, like how she hoped to be an author one day, her belief in God, what it was like to live under the cruelty of the Nazis.

In 1944, Anne and her family were captured, and in 1945, Anne died in a Nazi concentration camp. But Anne lives on today through her diary. In fact, before she died, Anne had already started to edit her diary so that it could be published—she wanted other peopled to know what it was like to live in the time of the Nazis. When the war was over, Anne's dad made it his mission to get his daughter's diary published. And in 1947, it was. In the following years, *Anne Frank: The Diary of a Young Girl* was translated into sixty-seven languages—and it's one of the most-read books in the entire world!

ACTIVITY 3:

Overhear Over There

"I wouldn't give it a canary." That's what I heard someone say the other day while I was waiting in line at the bookstore. I have no idea what it means. But it got my brain churning.

You can hear the greatest stuff—the only thing is, you really have to listen. And it's much easier to write realistic dialogue if you really listen to how people talk. So keep your

journal on hand and jot down bits of real conversation whenever you hear something good. Anywhere. Everywhere. At school. At the dentist. At a restaurant. In your kitchen. Then you can use different snips of conversations you heard throughout your writing—in stories, screenplays, poems, or whatever.

ACTIVITY 4:

Dream a Little Dream

Your dreams can tell you lots of stuff about what's going on inside your head. They can be funny, sad, scary, or all those things put together. So it's great to catch your dreams as soon as you can, so they don't slip away. That's why a dream journal is a totally great thing. I keep one right next to my bed, and whenever I have a dream I remember, I write it down right away. And the funny thing is, when you start writing about a dream, alotta times you start remembering all this stuff you didn't even remember you remembered.

Lots of writers use parts of their dreams in their writing. Choose a detail, a person, or an action from one of the dreams you've written about in your journal. Then try to use this piece of your dream in a poem, story, screenplay, or whatever in the space below. Like one time I dreamed I had two heads—I ended up writing a whole play around it (check out page 42 to read more about it).

ACTIVITY 5:
It's Automatic

Automatic writing is a cool thing my English teacher taught us recently. You just write down whatever words are in your head. They don't even have to make sense. And you write for however long you want. Alotta times when I do this, crazy other stuff comes out that I didn't even know was there. Okay, so I'll do it right now:

Bongo drum, kettle of fish, kitty litter, Chicken Little, spit, rain on my face, hey that reminds me I have to buy Jasmine a new umbrella, cuz I accidentally lost hers, it was raining I was at her house, and she lent me hers, but on the way home I stopped in at a totally fab art supply store, I love that place, I could spend hours in there, actually I did. So then I bought this crazy excellent shading pencil, and by the time I was done it stopped raining. And I totally left the umbrella at the art supply store.

I didn't even think about it until two days later, and then when I went back there it was gone. I felt really really really really horrible, but Jasmine is totally excellent about it. She's really good at accepting an apology. I'm trying to get better at that, I really am. Like the other day my sister said something really mean to me, and then she apologized later, but I wouldn't accept her apology. I wouldn't talk to her, I was such a sulky pill. That's definitely on my to-do list. To get better at accepting apologies.

So that's how automatic writing works! Now you try. Here is a page where you can let your mind wander.

chapter six:

the reporter
in me

Okay, before there were newspapers, and before the printing press was invented, people learned about the news through word-of-mouth. Like one big game of telephone! So you can imagine how totally twisted the news got back in the day. Sometimes news was told through letters (the problem with that was you had to be able to read and write, which not that many people knew how to do); through songs or ballads; or, like in medieval England, through a town crier. This was a dude who the town council paid to walk up and down the streets and yell at the top of his lungs, "Hear ye! Hear ye!" And then he would scream all the news that the people in charge wanted the rest of the citizens to know.

Governments used criers because most people couldn't read or write. The crier's announcements could be about what was going on in the government, like what kind of taxes you had to pay and when you had to pay them, or about the prince getting married—kind of like the front page of your newspaper. Or they could be about what days certain markets would be happening—kind of like the events page of your newspaper.

It wasn't until the seventeenth century that actual newspapers were published. And people seemed to love the idea. By 1800, there were like 230 newspapers published in the United States alone. Now there are kajillions of newspapers around the world, not to mention magazines, TV and radio stations that do news 24/7, blogs, and lots of other ways to find out what's going on. In other words, there are tons of places where reporters can get their work out there. So, if you're thinking about becoming a reporter, now is a great time to get the skinny on the whole thing.

I have been totally into reporting lately. About a year ago, a new girl named Margot moved to my town. Everybody thought she was kind of stuck up at first, but it turns out she's just sorta shy. Believe it or not, when I don't know someone I actually get an itty bitty bit shy myself. So I can totally relate.

Margot had been at school about a week and she was sitting by herself at lunch reading our school newspaper, so I thought, "What the heck?!" And I went and sat with her, even though I usually sit with Jasmine and Carla and Allison, and sometimes Megan and Melinda (they're twins). Margot was pretty quiet at first, but then we started talking about her mom, who's a reporter, and Margot got over her shyness crazy fast. So she told me that her mom is an investigative reporter. That's somebody who spends months or even years going after

a story about corruption, crime, or generally something evil going on in the world—because they wanna make it better. Margot's mom went to school to be a reporter, and Margot wants to be one when she's older, too.

Margot told me that a great reporter is like the ears, eyes, brain, heart, and conscience of the reader. Well, actually, Margot told me her mom said that. But I still think it's a really cool thing.

So now Margot eats lunch with all of us, and I met her mom when we had a sleepover. When I was at her house, Margot showed me this article her mom wrote about a mega-company that built these heinous cheap houses that kept falling apart. When you're reading the article, STG, it's like you can really see what these houses were like, and how horrible people's lives were because of their homes.

There was mold everywhere, so their kids got really sick; crummy plumbing that made the toilets overflow all the time; and really thin walls that made their heat so expensive in the winter that they couldn't afford to pay their bills. Lots and lots of owners complained, but the company wouldn't do anything about it—they thought they didn't have to because they were selling these junky houses to people who couldn't afford lawyers.

Margot's mom interviewed someone who used to work for the evil company and he showed her actual e-mails where the company talked about how easy it was to get away with what it was doing. Now, because of Margot's mom's article, there's a whole big trial with a famous judge and lots of other organizations helping all these people get brand-new homes—for free. How incredible is that?!

Anyway, I was so inspired by Margot's mom that I decided I would start doing some reporting for our school newspaper. I found out there were lots of types of reporters. Like, maybe you're not so into writing about crime or politics or other stuff you normally think is covered by the news. Maybe you love sports or fashion or traveling or interviewing famous or interesting people. Or maybe, instead, you love going to the movies, or reading books, or going out for dinner, and then talking about, and criticizing, and praising what you saw, read, or ate afterward. Then you might be a natural-born reviewer. No matter what you wanna do, there are pages of newspapers and magazines dedicated to writers just like you!

After reading the style section of my local paper, I decided to write my first article about a fashion show my sister was in (man, me and my sister got in a BIG fight about that one!). I also did some investigative reporting when I couldn't find the stickers I wanted at a local store, which I talked about before. And then I wrote about Jasmine's soccer team going to the regional championship.

Even though I haven't found any big, huge, terrible injustices I can write about yet, I keep looking. And so should you!

ACTIVITY 1:

Whatya Love?

A couple months ago, my dad was telling me about a journalist named Rachel Carson, who lived in the first part of the twentieth century. Lots of people say she started the environmental movement, which is something I'm really, totally, and completely

> **"One way to open your eyes is to ask yourself, 'What if I had never seen this before? What if I knew I would never see it again?'"**
>
> —Rachel Carson, author of *Silent Spring*

interested in. Anyway, my dad was saying what he loved about Rachel, and what got him inspired when he was a kid, was that she always wrote about things that she cared a ton about.

It turns out Rachel was wild for the wilderness. When she was a little kid, she would hang around ponds and forests, sitting with birds and insects for hours on end, trying to figure out what was going on in their world. And she loved to write about what she saw. She even got her first story published in a national magazine when she was just ten years old!

Rachel loved nature her whole life and ended up writing one of the most important books of the twentieth century: *Silent Spring*. The book helped the world understand that pesticides could be dangerous to the environment and to people. It started a whole movement to stop pesticide use and to take better care of the environment. Rachel actually changed the world by writing about what she loved.

So what in the world do you love? What do you wonder about? What do you think is interesting? Big stuff like global warming, or little stuff like why your cat has a scratchy tongue? What makes you agitated or angry? What makes you ridiculously happy? Now make a list of stuff like that here. This is your master story list. It will help you decide what you wanna write about as you pursue your career as a reporter.

You can begin by looking for stories that are about these general topics. Like, if you love pooches, you might wanna write a profile about the dashing dalmation that won the Westminster Dog Show. Or if you love to cook, like me, and you go to a super-great new

Indian restaurant, you could write a review or even a profile of the owners. It's crazy, but when I started looking around, I realized that there are stories everywhere—you just gotta know what you're looking for!

Story ideas:

1. _____

2. _____

3. _____

4. _____

5. _____

6. _____

7. _____

8. _____

9. _____

10. _____

ACTIVITY 2:
Interview Overview

Being a great reporter is all about getting your facts straight. And you can't get your facts straight if you don't ask lots of questions. Margot's mom even told me that at the school she went to, they had a saying that goes like this: "If your mother says she loves you, check it out!" In other words, never trust just one person (or "source" as he or she is called in reporter lingo). Always confirm a fact that you read or hear by interviewing more than one person or by looking up the information in more than one place. That's why, if you wanna be a reporter, you have to learn how to interview people.

Interviews are how you find out the info you need for your story. It's better not to ask questions that someone can answer with just "yes" or "no."

LMM tip

Did your interviewee tell you that she had her milk delivered to her door in glass bottles as a kid? But do you remember your grandma saying that this stopped happening in your town long before your interviewee said? Check the facts! Interview other people around her age, look it up on the Internet, go to your local historical society, or ask a librarian!

Instead, Margot's mom says you should ask open-ended questions like: How do you feel about global warming? What do you think is cool about a cat's tongue? And if someone is having a hard time talking to you, it's usually good to just chitchat first. This helps people feel comfortable.

Ready for your first interview? One of my favorites is to interview the oldest person you know. This could be a grandparent, your neighbor, or an old lady you see at the park all the time. You can start with some obvious questions, like, When and where were you born?, or Where did you go to school? But make sure to also ask about stuff that will let your interviewee open up and talk, like, How has the world changed since when you were a kid?, or What are some of the most amazing things you've ever seen? I also ask questions like, What are some of the smartest things people ever said to you?, or What is the most ridiculous thing that ever happened to you? Be sure to try out my personal favorite: What's the worst thing you ever got in trouble for? You can take notes on your interview here.

ACTIVITY 3:

Staking Out the Scene of the Crime

Let's say you're writing an article for your school newspaper about how a big window on the second floor broke. Most people are saying it was because someone threw a rock up there from the top of the fence around the schoolyard. If you wanna be a superstar reporter, then you wouldn't just write what people were saying. No way José! You'd climb up to the top of the fence and measure the distance to see if it was even possible to throw that far. When you discovered that there's no way that could happen, then you'd go to the janitor and ask him what he saw the day that the window broke. When he tells you that the only thing that he remembers is that the lock was off the back door when he got to work, then you

might start to wonder if somebody broke the window from the inside, not the outside.

If it was broken from the inside, then there might still be glass on the ground below the window outside. So then you'd start searching down there. And when you find a sliver that resembles the glass in the window, well then, my friend, you've just become a superstar reporter. Because you went to the scene of the crime and you pulled out your fine-tooth comb.

Going to the scene of the crime doesn't actually totally literally mean "the scene of the crime." Because there's probably not going to be any crime involved (and if there is, then you probably wanna stay away!). It just means going to the place where the action happened. To get really good at looking around and learning about the scene of an event, find a mystery in your house and write down anything and everything you can see about how this mystery could have happened.

Like, I've always wanted to know where missing socks go. First, you put them in the laundry bin, then you put 'em in the washer. If you're lucky, they're still around when it's time to put them in the dryer, but after that, they just disappear! So where in the world do these socks go? First I asked myself, "If I were a sock, where would I go?" With that in my head, I went to the laundry room and thought, "Yeah, if I were a sock, I might be behind the storage bins and the huge toolbox." Right off the bat, I found three missing socks.

I kept saying, "If I were a sock, where would I go?!" Then, I got a flashlight and searched behind the washer and dryer. Two more

lost socks were found. Someone had once told me that socks can get caught in your dryer's pipe. So I begged my mom to ask the handyman who was over fixing our dishwasher to undo the pipe. Fifteen socks!!! I found twenty socks in all, and one was one of my ATFs: my purple and green star sock.

You, too, might discover a long-lost friend as you hunt down your story. So find your own mystery, investigate, and then write about it here.

ACTIVITY 4:

The Five *Ws* and a Lonely *H*

Go to an event where you think something crazy, kooky, marvelous, wild, or interesting is going to happen—a poetry reading, carnival, save-the-environment rally, whatever. While you're there, take totally excellent notes about the five *W*s and the lonely *H*: That's the *who, what, when, where, why,* and *how.* The more details you notice, the better. And be super-specific. Like, write down that the "best pie" in the carnival was in a bubble-gum-pink ceramic dish with little bits of blueberry spilling onto the edges and crystals of sugar sprinkled on top. Mmm, now I'm super-duper hungry. See how details work?

Now, write an article based on your notes. Go through each question and make sure you put all the answers in your article: *Who* was there? *What* happened, from the little stuff people did, to the bigger stuff, like what was the main event? *Where* did it happen, what were the surroundings? *When* was it, like what time and which day of the week? *Why* was everybody there, why did everything happen the way it did? And *how* did everything go down? Was there a plan or did it all just fall into place? Use this exercise for every article you write. Trust me, it'll really help!

Who
_____
_____
_____
_____
_____

What

Where

When

Why

How

ACTIVITY 5:

Inverted Pyramids

When you tell your friends stories, they usually roll out something like, "Listen to this! I was sitting minding my own business, when so-and-so walked up and said blah-blah-blah, and then this happened, and then this happened, and then this happened, and then, can you believe it, it ended like this!" Well, in the reporter racket, your readers don't have time for all that. They're on the go, tying their shoes, slurping their cereal, and packing their bags, all while reading your article about the thing that happened to you when you were minding your own business.

If you don't grab people in your first paragraph (which is called a "lead"), then you'll never get them to read the rest of your story, no matter how juicy it is. So, it's every reporter's job to lure in readers with a tantalizing lead, something jam-packed with all the most essential information, as well as words that pump up the drama. Here are two solid leads from *The New York Times*:

> *"The eldest children in families tend to develop slightly higher I.Q.s than their younger siblings, researchers are reporting, based on a large study that could effectively settle more than a half-century of scientific debate about the relationship between I.Q. and birth order."*

> —from "Study Says Eldest Children Have Higher I.Q.s," by Benedict Carey

> *"The plain metal rowboats at the Central Park Boathouse are surprisingly similar to the skiff that Bear Grylls commandeered in Alaska during an episode of* Man vs. Wild, *his hit series on the Discovery Channel. Except that his leaked, lacked oars and eventually sank among a pack of ice floes, forcing him to strip down to a T-shirt and swim to shore. The*

water was so frigid that he started hyperventilating as his pulse raced to the heart-attack zone."

—from "Are You Tough Enough? An Adventurer's Guide to Surviving the Wilds," by Patricia Cohen

The first is an example of a straight lead—just the facts, ma'am—and the second is an example of a feature lead, in which interesting details and tension are used to draw in readers. The first example is what reporters use for breaking news (news that's happening right this moment), and the second is what reporters use when the story isn't necessarily breaking news, but will be interesting to readers.

While the lead is super-important because it sets the tone for everything else to come in the story, these other components are essential, too.

❋ **The Body**: Here's where you discuss all the *W*s and the lonely *H* in depth. The body is where you work in your best quotes from people you interviewed and try to answer all the questions you've raised. You may describe characters and places, and you may have to say something like "Jo Bob was not available for comment" if you tried to reach a source but couldn't. This is the meat and potatoes section of your story, where readers go to find out more about what you promised in the lead paragraph.

In most news stories the most important information comes first and the least important information last— this is called the "inverted pyramid." Go ahead and draw a pyramid on a blank paper. Now turn the paper so the tip of the pyramid is pointing down. The tip of the pyramid has the

LMM tip

Wanna see your very own words in the newspaper sooner rather than later? You can! But first you have to read the paper to know what's going on. You don't have to read the whole thing, but try to read at least one article a day in the sections you're interested in. Okay, so how's this gonna help you get published? The easiest way to get your foot in the door is to write a letter to the editor or to write an editorial. In order to write a letter, you have to be responding to an article you've read. And in order to write an editorial, you have to know what's going on in the news at the moment.

One last thing: If you send in a letter or editorial, make sure to include your age. Editors really enjoy hearing from kids like us!

least important detail in the story (like the color of the chair you were sitting in when so and so bumped into you), and the fat base of the pyramid, now at the top, has all the important stuff—the *W*s and the *H* and the juiciest details and quotes.

❁ **The Kicker or Conclusion:** Sometimes news stories end on way dull notes, especially when they use the inverted pyramid, where the least important info is shoved into paragraphs at the end of a story. But sometimes, especially in non-news stories, it's fun to end with something that sums up your article or captures what your story is really about. It might be a fun fact, a killer quote, or a question the article raises. Like, the feature lead by Patricia Cohen that I mentioned before led to a great story about how this dude survived in the wild and ended by talking about how he had to drink his own pee to survive! Eeeeeeew!!!

So you've figured out what you love and gone after it. You've gathered the interviews and determined the *W*s and the *H*. And you've got all your notes in a stack and you're ready to write your article. Now use all the info to construct your story in the space below. That way, the rest of us can read all about it!

conclusion

If you're like me, you'll go gaga over all the stuff that comes in this kit. My favorite thing is probably the dream journal. That's cuz I have such wacky madcap dreams, and, unless I write them down, they drift away like clouds on a summer day.

Actually the travel journal might be my favorite of all because I love taking trips, near or far, with my friends and my family . . . or even by myself. And the travel journal is so petite that I can take it with me wherever I go.

Well, now that I think about it, my favorite thing in this box may be the diary. STG, if I don't write in my diary for a couple of days, I start to get all goofy and moody.

Hold on a second . . . I think I like the reporter notebook the most cuz I can record all the details of a story in the making— right at the scene of the crime.

Wow, sorry, I just realized that what I really love the best are my wild word cards. I have collected some of the most fabulously fabulous words, and use them whenever I want to write a new poem.

Oh! I just remembered how much I adore my Write On! poster that is hanging on the wall in my room. With quotes from some of the greatest women writers of all time, it inspires me whenever I can't think of the right thing to write.

You know, to be completely truthful, I love EVERYTHING in this kit, and I know you will too. I really hope that it helps you find the writer in you!